FORUM ON Cyber Resilience
WORKSHOP SERIES

Recoverability as a First-Class Security Objective

PROCEEDINGS OF A WORKSHOP

Anne Frances Johnson and Lynette I. Millett, *Rapporteurs*

The National Academies of
SCIENCES · ENGINEERING · MEDICINE

THE NATIONAL ACADEMIES PRESS
Washington, DC
www.nap.edu

The National Academies of
SCIENCES · ENGINEERING · MEDICINE

The **National Academy of Sciences** was established in 1863 by an Act of Congress, signed by President Lincoln, as a private, nongovernmental institution to advise the nation on issues related to science and technology. Members are elected by their peers for outstanding contributions to research. Dr. Marcia McNutt is president.

The **National Academy of Engineering** was established in 1964 under the charter of the National Academy of Sciences to bring the practices of engineering to advising the nation. Members are elected by their peers for extraordinary contributions to engineering. Dr. C. D. Mote, Jr., is president.

The **National Academy of Medicine** (formerly the Institute of Medicine) was established in 1970 under the charter of the National Academy of Sciences to advise the nation on medical and health issues. Members are elected by their peers for distinguished contributions to medicine and health. Dr. Victor J. Dzau is president.

The three Academies work together as the **National Academies of Sciences, Engineering, and Medicine** to provide independent, objective analysis and advice to the nation and conduct other activities to solve complex problems and inform public policy decisions. The National Academies also encourage education and research, recognize outstanding contributions to knowledge, and increase public understanding in matters of science, engineering, and medicine.

Learn more about the National Academies of Sciences, Engineering, and Medicine at www.nationalacademies.org.

COMMITTEE ON CYBER RESILIENCE WORKSHOP SERIES

FRED B. SCHNEIDER, NAE,[1] Cornell University, *Chair*
ANITA ALLEN, NAM,[2] University of Pennsylvania
ERIC GROSSE, Independent Consultant
BUTLER W. LAMPSON, NAS[3]/NAE, Microsoft Corporation
SUSAN LANDAU, Worcester Polytechnic Institute

Staff

LYNETTE I. MILLETT, Director, Forum on Cyber Resilience
EMILY GRUMBLING, Program Officer
SHENAE BRADLEY, Senior Program Assistant

---

[1] National Academy of Engineering.
[2] National Academy of Medicine.
[3] National Academy of Sciences.

FORUM ON CYBER RESILIENCE

FRED B. SCHNEIDER, NAE, Cornell University, *Chair*
ANITA ALLEN, NAM, University of Pennsylvania
ROBERT BLAKLEY, Citigroup
FRED CATE, Indiana University
DAVID D. CLARK, NAE, Massachusetts Institute of Technology
RICHARD DANZIG, Johns Hopkins University
ERIC GROSSE, Independent Consultant
DAVID HOFFMAN, Intel Corporation
PAUL KOCHER, Independent Researcher
TADAYOSHI KOHNO, University of Washington
BUTLER W. LAMPSON, NAS/NAE, Microsoft Corporation
SUSAN LANDAU, Tufts University
STEVEN B. LIPNER, NAE, SAFECode
JOHN MANFERDELLI, Northeastern University
DEIRDRE K. MULLIGAN, University of California, Berkeley
TONY SAGER, Center for Internet Security
WILLIAM SANDERS, University of Illinois at Urbana-Champaign
PETER SWIRE, Georgia Institute of Technology
DAVID VLADECK, Georgetown University
MARY ELLEN ZURKO, MIT Lincoln Laboratory

Ex Officio
DONNA DODSON, National Institute for Standards and Technology
JEREMY EPSTEIN, National Science Foundation
WILLIAM MARTIN, National Security Agency

Staff
LYNETTE I. MILLETT, Director
EMILY GRUMBLING, Program Officer
KATIRIA ORTIZ, Associate Program Officer
SHENAE BRADLEY, Administrative Assistant

For more information about the Forum, see its website at http://www.cyber-forum.org, or e-mail the Forum at cyberforum@nas.edu.

COMPUTER SCIENCE AND TELECOMMUNICATIONS BOARD

FARNAM JAHANIAN, Carnegie Mellon University, *Chair*
LUIZ ANDRE BARROSO, Google, Inc.
STEVEN M. BELLOVIN, NAE, Columbia University
ROBERT F. BRAMMER, Brammer Technology, LLC
EDWARD FRANK, Cloud Parity, Inc.
LAURA HAAS, NAE, University of Massachusetts, Amherst
MARK HOROWITZ, NAE, Stanford University
ERIC HORVITZ, NAE, Microsoft Research
VIJAY KUMAR, NAE, Univ. of Pennsylvania
BETH MYNATT, Georgia Institute of Technology
CRAIG PARTRIDGE, Raytheon BBN Technologies
DANIELA RUS, NAE, Massachusetts Institute of Technology
FRED B. SCHNEIDER, NAE, Cornell University
MARGO SELTZER, Harvard University
MOSHE VARDI, NAS/NAE, Rice University
KATHERINE YELICK, University of California, Berkeley

Staff
JON EISENBERG, Senior Director
LYNETTE I. MILLETT, Associate Director

SHENAE BRADLEY, Administrative Assistant
EMILY GRUMBLING, Program Officer
RENEE HAWKINS, Financial and Administrative Manager
KATIRIA ORTIZ, Associate Program Officer
JANKI PATEL, Senior Program Assistant

For more information on CSTB, see its website at http://www.cstb.org, write to CSTB, National Research Council, 500 Fifth Street, NW, Washington, DC 20001, call (202) 334-2605, or email the CSTB at cstb@nas.edu.

ACKNOWLEDGMENT OF REVIEWERS

This Proceedings of a Workshop was reviewed in draft form by individuals chosen for their diverse perspectives and technical expertise. The purpose of this independent review is to provide candid and critical comments that will assist the National Academies of Sciences, Engineering, and Medicine in making each published proceedings as sound as possible and to ensure that it meets the institutional standards for quality, objectivity, evidence, and responsiveness to the charge. The review comments and draft manuscript remain confidential to protect the integrity of the process.
We thank the following individuals for their review of this proceedings:

Robert Blakley, Citigroup, Inc.,
Steven B. Lipner, NAE,[1] SAFECode,
Peter G. Neumann, SRI International, and
Tony W. Sager, Center for Internet Security.

Although the reviewers listed above provided many constructive comments and suggestions, they were not asked to endorse the content of the proceedings nor did they see the final draft before its release. The review of this proceedings was overseen by Steven M. Bellovin, NAE, Columbia University. He was responsible for making certain that an independent examination of this proceedings was carried out in accordance with standards of the National Academies and that all review comments were carefully considered. Responsibility for the final content rests entirely with the rapporteurs and the National Academies.

---
[1] National Academy of Engineering.

Preface

The Forum on Cyber Resilience—a roundtable established in 2015 by the National Academies of Sciences, Engineering, and Medicine—facilitates and enhances the exchange of ideas among scientists, practitioners, and policy makers who are concerned with urgent and important issues related to the resilience of the nation's computing and communications systems, including the Internet, other critical infrastructures, and commercial systems. Forum activities help inform and engage a broad range of stakeholders around issues involving technology and policy related to cyber resilience, cybersecurity, privacy, and related emerging issues. A key role for the forum is to surface and explore topics that advance the national conversation.

In 2016, the forum held a workshop to explore the topic of mitigating harms from data breach. That workshop was summarized in *Data Breach Aftermath and Recovery for Individuals and Institutions: Proceedings of a Workshop.* Discussions during and subsequent to that workshop highlighted how cyberattacks and breaches can also compromise availability and/or integrity of critical systems. The abilities to mitigate the effects of a successful attack and to reliably recover—either to full functionality or to a well-understood set of critical functionalities—are important; in some circumstances, recovering to full functionality is more important than protecting confidentiality.

To explore recoverability as a first-class security objective—at different granularities (from documents to data centers) and from both research and operational perspectives—the forum decided to host a workshop. The workshop featured invited speakers from the government, private sector, and academia. This proceedings summarizes presentations made by invited speakers and other remarks by workshop participants. In keeping with the workshop's exploratory purpose, the proceedings does not contain findings or recommendations. Nor, in keeping with National Academies guidelines for workshop proceedings, does it necessarily report consensus views of the workshop participants or organizing committee. The planning group appointed to oversee all forum workshops was limited to planning the workshop, and this workshop proceedings was prepared by the workshop rapporteurs and forum staff as a factual summary of what occurred at the workshop. The document draws on prepared remarks of workshop speakers, comments made by workshop participants, and ensuing discussions.

The first chapter summarizes the introduction to the workshop, reproduces background material provided to all participants, and summarizes the introductory keynote by Butler Lampson. Chapter 2 summarizes speaker presentations. Chapter 3 describes the content of the final plenary discussion, highlighting some of the broader themes that emerged throughout the workshop. The agenda of the workshop is in Appendix A, and short biosketches of the planning group and speakers appear in Appendixes B and C, respectively.

My sincere thanks to the planning group, forum members, and staff who helped organize the workshop, as well as to the invited speakers for their thoughtful remarks and enthusiastic participation in the discussions that ensued. Writing support was provided by Anne Frances Johnson and Kathleen Pierce, Creative Science Writing. I also extend our appreciation to the National Science Foundation and the National Security Agency and the Special Cyber Operations Research and Engineering Working Group, and the National Institute of Standards and Technology for their support and encouragement of forum activities.

Fred B. Schneider, *Chair*
Forum on Cyber Resilience

Contents

1 INTRODUCTION AND FRAMING   1
    Opening Remarks   1
    Framing Keynote: A Broad View of Recovery   2

2 SUMMARY OF WORKSHOP PRESENTATIONS   9
    The Role of Trust in Breach Recovery   9
    Resilience in the U.S. Financial Sector   14
    Resilience the Amazon Way   16
    Resilience and Recovery in the Electric Grid   20
    Community Resilience and the Framework for Improving
        Critical Infrastructure for Cybersecurity   23

3 CLOSING OBSERVATIONS AND DISCUSSION   28
    Closing Observations   28
    Closing Plenary Discussion   30

APPENDIXES   37
    A   Workshop Agenda and Participants List   38
    B   Planning Committee Biographies   40
    C   Speaker Biographies   43

Introduction and Framing

The Forum on Cyber Resilience of the National Academies of Sciences, Engineering, and Medicine hosted the Workshop on Recoverability as a First-Class Security Objective on February 8, 2018, in Washington, D.C.

The workshop featured presentations from several experts in industry, research, and government roles who spoke about the complex facets of recoverability—that is, the ability to restore normal operations and security in a system affected by software or hardware failure or a deliberate attack. The workshop concluded with a lively discussion of the presentations, the uncertainties and complexities involved, and ideas for future research on resilience and recovery.

The meeting was open to the public. This proceedings was created from the presenters' slides and a full transcript of the meeting and is intended to serve as a public record of the workshop presentations and discussions.

OPENING REMARKS

Fred B. Schneider, Forum Chair

Fred Schneider, the Samuel B. Eckert Professor of Computer Science at Cornell University, member of the National Academy of Engineering, and workshop chair, opened the meeting with an overview of the National Academies' Forum on Cyber Resilience.

Forum workshops are designed to bring together experts in relevant fields to share their perspectives on issues that the forum views as critical topics in cyber infrastructure and cyber resilience. The forum takes a deliberately wide view of cyber infrastructure as it relates to technology's increasingly ubiquitous presence in our lives. Workshops typically address both technical and policy implications of selected topics.

This workshop's focus was on recovery of technological systems after a failure or intrusion. While it may seem mundane, recoverability is much more complicated than most people realize, and a lack of recoverability can have severe consequences, Schneider said. The purpose of the workshop's presentations and discussions is to probe the issue deeply by identifying key recovery issues and understanding their importance, both within the technology world and for the wider public.

FRAMING KEYNOTE: A BROAD VIEW OF RECOVERY

Butler W. Lampson, Microsoft Research

Butler Lampson, technical fellow at Microsoft Research, kicked off the workshop with a keynote address framing the issue of recovery. He took a broad view of recovery, discussing its meaning and implications, its role within cybersecurity, and pathways for improvement.

Recoverability Scope and Goals

Recovery is a vital component of cybersecurity because it provides a means to move forward after breaches and successful attacks occur. Software bugs, hardware failures, and deliberate attacks can affect all types of systems, making recoverability relevant not only for cloud or server systems but also for end-user items such as personal computers, phones, and Internet of Things (IoT) devices.

Lampson described a successful recovery as follows: A *successful r*ecovery regains a system's availability, integrity, and confidentiality. First, normal service should be made available quickly.[1] Second, the software and hardware should be returned to a state of integrity that is both safe and current—attributes that can be difficult to achieve at the same time. Finally, it is important to restore confidentiality, although once secrets have been made public, preventing subsequent access to them entirely can be very difficult, if not impossible.

---

[1] In some contexts, returning to a state of degraded or minimum essential services may be an important interim step toward normal service.

Recasting Recovery within Cybersecurity

Lampson noted that most consider the goal of cybersecurity efforts and practices to be to prevent intrusions and their negative consequences. Although this is a worthy goal, he noted that in his view, it is nearly impossible to prevent all intrusions. He posited that it may be more effective, and more realistic, to pursue two other security goals simultaneously—to recover easily from security breaches and to punish attackers. Indeed, many of the steps taken toward prevention can also assist in recovery efforts (e.g., inventory control of hardware and software, logging and monitoring strategies, and so on). These goals, recovery and accountability, place greater emphasis on deterrence, representing what Lampson calls a "retroactive" view of security. In combination, accountability coupled with recovery (which limits the impacts of an attack, thereby making it a less attractive course) may help deter bad actors.

Current cybersecurity approaches provide some minimal facilities for prevention and recovery, such as securing simple programs and isolating complex programs or sanitizing their inputs. However, Lampson said current approaches fall short in securing more complex systems or maintaining security after changes are made. He also observed that users cannot be expected to be skilled or informed enough to make good security decisions, which further compounds the challenge.

Lampson noted that the standard approach to cybersecurity is to isolate a system, limit access to it, and include a software guard that monitors access attempts. He observed that in theory, this setup prevents security breaches, but we know that in practice, it does not always work. These experiences, he argued, suggest a need to change how we perceive and pursue security goals.

First, instead of trying to secure everything, Lampson posited that we should prioritize what is truly important. He used the analogy of a bank vault—they are expensive and inconvenient but work very well for storing the most valuable items. Second, instead of trying to prevent all possible attacks, we should be reacting to actual attacks and focusing on deterrence and recovery, which is largely how security is tackled in the non-cyber world. Burglars, he noted, are not dissuaded by complex household locks but rather by the fear of jail time.

Retroactive security may not be perfect, but it is better than the current system, Lampson argued. It does not mean that there are no bugs in the code, it means that people who take advantage of the bugs get punished. In fact, according to Lampson, the aspects of current cybersecurity approaches that work well often draw their value from retroactive measures, such as the ability to undo fraudulent financial transactions.

Background and Context

The following information was provided to workshop speakers and attendees to offer context on recoverability issues and to provide a structure for the workshop and its intended purposes.

Large-scale data breaches have spotlighted the challenge of maintaining confidentiality of data.[1] Cyberattacks and breaches, such as ransomware, can also compromise availability and/or integrity of critical systems. The abilities to mitigate the effects of a successful attack and to reliably recover either to full functionality, or to a well-understood set of critical functionalities, are important; in some circumstances, recovering to full functionality is more important than the ability to protect confidentiality. This workshop will explore such **recoverability** as a first-class security objective—at different granularities (from documents to data centers) and from both research and operational perspectives.

A long history of cybersecurity challenges and failures suggests that preventing attacks, although important, is insufficient. Attacks will sometimes succeed, and we must be able to return a system to operation confidently and expeditiously after the attack has been detected. The security policies, practices, and implementations for most information systems today are not designed to facilitate recoverability. What would constitute an effective approach to recovery is likely to be system- and domain-specific. For some systems, complete functionality might need to be restored rapidly. For most systems, however, it may suffice to have cataloged which capabilities are critical (for instance, read access to files in cloud storage or SMS capabilities on a phone might be deemed critical) and then continually to update plans and processes that ensure those capabilities can be rapidly recovered.[2]

In financial services, for example, relatively clear guidelines have been established. For instance, contractual agreements are put in place that describe expectations and impose penalties when those expectations are not met. In addition, most financial transactions can be undone if need be, back-up data systems are isolated, and so on. In other contexts, similar thought is nascent. Discussion of power grid cyber resilience and associated restart capabilities, for example, is only now intensifying.

Support for system recoverability, requires new research, new tools, and new practices. Recoverability can be addressed at many levels of granularity in a system—from processes and practices that provide for ready recovery of data in an enterprise environment to large-scale transparent fail-overs or priority-feature provisions to millions of users for a web application.

Support for data recovery is often important part of overall system recoverability. After an intrusion, system operators and users may be left uncertain about:

- Whether intruders have actually been evicted from the system,
- What data can be trusted and what data may have been altered,

---

[1] In 2016, the Forum on Cyber Resilience hosted a workshop on mitigating harms from data breach. A summary of discussions at that workshop is available from National Academies of Sciences, Engineering, and Medicine, *Data Breach Aftermath and Recovery for Individuals and Institutions: Proceedings of a Workshop,* The National Academies Press, Washington, DC, 2016, https://doi.org/10.17226/23559.

[2] R. Danzig, *Surviving on a Diet of Poisoned Fruit: Reducing the National Security Risks of America's Cyber Dependencies,* Center for a New American Security, Washington, DC, July 2014; B. Lampson, "Viewpoint: Usable Security—How to Get It," *Comm.* ACM 52(11:25-27, 2009.

- How far in the past the intrusion occurred and thus how far the system must be backed up, and/or
- Whether intruders have installed back doors that will facilitate their return.

Operationally, there is much to learn regarding how better to recover from attacks, outages, and failures. DevOps and system administration communities have an important role to play in improving the recoverability of systems.

Topics speakers at the workshop will be invited to address:

Policies and Practices
- How to design effective organizational policies, terms of service, and/or guarantees that provide sufficient incentive for services to reliably recover from disruption; what policy and organizational changes help to improve recoverability prospects?
- What aspects of the legal, policy, and regulatory landscape affect requirements for recoverability? For example, e-discovery rules, by which parties are expected to share documents electronically, has implications for how information systems that support legal efforts are designed and architected.
- What data and metadata are needed to effectively recover after a widespread ransomware or destructive malware incident in an enterprise?
- Examples of recovery approaches at a variety of scales (documents to data centers) and for various kind of security properties; case studies. To what extent can learning and insights from these experiences be generalized to be accessible to others who wish to develop better recoverability prospects?
- Cyber recoverability in practice—what can we learn from DevOps and SysAdmin communities about bringing systems and capabilities back online after a breach or failure?
- In addition to technical recovery what plans and processes can help recover from failures of trust (for instance, a significant certificate authority is breached, with revelation of the private signing key)?
- What kinds of advance preparation are useful to help response plans be more effective?

Learning from Other Domains
- What would be the digital infrastructure equivalent of a power grid "black start"? What is the equivalent of "safe mode" while in recovery? Can recovery of all or part of an on-premises configuration be quickly recovered to a public cloud environment, and what preparation would be needed to make this possible?
- Assessing recoverability needs—what are the critical aspects and how can those be determined? For instance, how do organizations (or industries/sectors) prioritize between repairing damage versus providing services? What non-digital processes and capabilities aid digital recovery? How are recovery efforts complicated when IoT devices are involved?
- What lessons can be learned from other industries and sectors related to community resilience and disaster response and recovery?

Research
Research that is required to facilitate recovery, including problem formulation, coping with various scale dimensions, and addressing system administration and configuration as first-class security research considerations.

Foundations for Recoverability

Lampson argued that in order for retroactive security to work, there needs to be a solid and secure core of the given system that can reboot to a clean state after a breach, that can verify signatures of both regular distributions and patches, and that can capture an audit log to determine where problems have occurred. The core should be able to perform updates to that clean state based on a redo log, which is preferable to a system-wide backup (where work could be lost). He noted that there should also be a secure configuration, with a list of acceptable software and trusted principals who have access to it. In addition, audit logs and user authentication can be used to detect unusual behavior.

Lampson explained that in addition to helping restore the system to a good state, these foundational elements enable accountability, and ultimately blame, so that offenders can be found and punished, whether with jail time, fines, being fired, or some other accountability measure. Lampson said that if widely implemented, a secure foundation could handle small annoyances, such as spam, as well as larger problems, such as a major security breach by a state-sponsored actor.

Today, restoring the integrity of a system as part of recovery is often very difficult and time intensive. Lampson pointed to the work of Taesoo Kim, Georgia Institute of Technology, as a promising direction in which to head. Kim and his colleagues propose an approach based on the notion of "selective redo" or "selective undo," where only the bad acts and their consequences are undone during recovery and restoration. He said their research demonstrates that selective undo can significantly improve recoverability in a variety of scenarios.[2]

Confidentiality also suffers when systems are breached, and secrets cannot be retrieved once publicly revealed. However, Lampson observed, secrets can be protected in ways that make them harder to find, an approach pursued in Europe under the "right to be forgotten" approach. Or, he said, confidentiality could be enhanced by stricter enforcement of rules regarding the use of data, such as by implementing identity tags and other mechanisms to build a chain of data tracking and handling within those systems that are under the purview of effective government regulation. Implementing such measures more widely would be difficult, but well worth the effort, Lampson argued.

Special Considerations for Internet of Things

Lampson then turned to the IoT, which he said is especially problematic with regard to cybersecurity. Unlike traditional computers, IoT devices are embedded in the real world where they have physical world impacts, and the business models behind most

---

[2] T. Kim et al., "Intrusion Recovery Using Selective Re-Execution," *Proceedings of the 9th Symposium on Operating Systems Design and Implementation*, 2010.

IoT devices result in millions of lines of code being written by inexpert programmers. In addition, update capabilities are often not as robust as in other sorts of systems, making recovery from malicious modification more challenging. The consequences of failure in these devices can be serious; malfunctions in a "smart" traffic light, for example, could cause major traffic accidents.

To address such challenges, Lampson proposed several approaches IoT companies could take. First, it could be useful to increase the emphasis on building IoT devices from common components that are thoroughly tested and formally verified, rather than separate, made-to-order components for each device. Second, Lampson urged that "safety-critical code" be identified and isolated for even stricter testing. An extension of this approach, he said, is to architecturally separate safety-critical code from non-critical code. In a smart traffic light, for example, safety critical code would tell the lights to always be red in at least one direction, and to stay yellow for 3 seconds before switching to red. The code for other, less critical functions of the light could be physically separate from these critical code components and not be able to override the safety-critical code. Lampson noted that while such approaches are feasible in a smaller system such as a traffic light, implementing them in more complex IoT devices, such as self-driving cars, will be more challenging.

Questions and Discussion

Lampson concluded by posing several questions for attendees to consider throughout the workshop:

- Can the recoverability strengths of the biggest cloud services, which are thought to be the most secure, be scaled down for smaller systems?

- Can we better incentivize design for recovery and make selective undo more practical?

- Is there an easier way to prevent secrets from being published?

- Finally, how do we know whether our current foundations are strong enough to allow for good recovery?

In closing, Lampson emphasized that recovery is a vital component of cybersecurity and that answering such questions will be important to devising effective solutions.

Tadayoshi Kohno, University of Washington, asked whether a shared definition of recovery exists and where researchers should focus their efforts, given the many challenges in this space and the many dimensions of recovery, such as timing, effects on interconnected systems, and the needs of different stakeholders. Lampson said that in his view, recovery is restoring system software or hardware to a good, current state while continuing to deliver service.

With regard to the challenge of preventing breaches of confidentiality, Susan Landau, Tufts University, noted that the HTTPA protocol, developed by a team of Massachusetts Institute of Technology researchers, explored an approach to establishing data provenance for various purposes, including for tracking privacy or copyright violations.

Peter Swire, Georgia Institute of Technology, pointed out that other domains, such as counterterrorism, are moving toward emphasizing prevention rather than punishment—the opposite of the retroactive approach Lampson proposes. It is a comfortable myth to believe that our lives or our computers and devices can be made fully secure, Lampson said, but it is not possible to prevent all threats from being realized. Focusing on prevention, he argued, perpetuates the myth of security, while focusing on recovery and punishment represents a more realistic view.

2

Summary of Workshop Presentations

THE ROLE OF TRUST IN BREACH RECOVERY

Heather Adkins, Google, Inc.

Heather Adkins, director of information security and privacy at Google, Inc., shared an on-the-ground perspective of recoverability based on her nearly 20 years of experience as a security practitioner. At Google, Adkins's realm is primarily in remediation. The chief information officer, information technology administrators, and site reliability engineers (SREs) who handle tactical and strategic recovery when necessary would all offer a different perspective on these issues, she noted.

Weaknesses of Current Responses

Adkins began with the caveat that she, and the vast majority of her in-the-trenches peers, do not closely follow, and in some cases are unfamiliar with, National Institute of Standards and Technology (NIST) Special Publication (SP) 800-184, *Guide for Cybersecurity Event Recovery*.[1] Although she believes the standard contains excellent advice for an ideal world, she asserted that the day-to-day reality is very different from

---

[1] M. Bartock et al., *Guide for Cybersecurity Event Recovery*, NIST SP 800-184, National Institute of Standards and Technology, Gaithersburg, MD, 2016, https://csrc.nist.gov/publications/detail/sp/800-184/final.

the world the standard seems to assume and that implementing the guidelines would be impractical for already overworked security teams.

In addition to being unable to fully implement ideal practices, Adkins posited that on-the-ground recovery teams are hampered by the fact that several common recovery strategies are actually weaker than one would like to think. For example, even seasoned first responders are known to run antivirus software to detect and remove problems, but these programs cannot detect or address advanced threats. In addition, if malicious files are spotted and removed in response, attackers can notice the change and switch tactics instead of retreating. Rebuilding a system also may be ineffective, because it merely drives an attacker to wreak havoc in another part of the network.

> Several common recovery strategies are weaker than one would like to think.

Quarantining a compromised network is another common recovery strategy, but it can backfire if someone unwittingly plugs it back into the active network again—a scenario Adkins has seen in practice. Similarly, shutting down a virtual machine that has been hacked seems reasonable, but avenues to these machines can remain open, so they also are at risk of being restarted. In scenarios involving a password breach, while password resetting can stop active hijacking, it might be too late to stop any processes an attacker may have set in motion while they had access.

Adkins described a well-known 2011 compromise of the systems that hosted Linux kernel development[2] in which hackers eventually damaged the system so badly that it was beyond recovery and had to be rebuilt. This example is particularly worrisome because Linux code is pervasive in billions of devices. Police were able to arrest one of the hackers, a breakthrough that offered some insights into the scope of the compromise and methods used, but the technical response and recovery effort was enormous, including the painstaking verification of 15 million lines of code to identify any remaining back doors.[3] In the context of this example, Adkins agreed with Butler Lampson's (Microsoft Research) earlier assertion that selective undo is appealing (and could in theory have offered a way to streamline the recovery), but she noted that the approach

---

[2] See U.S. Attorney's Office, Northern District of California, "Florida Computer Programmer Arrested for Hacking," Press Release, September 1, 2016, https://www.justice.gov/usao-ndca/pr/florida-computer-programmer-arrested-hacking, and the indictment in the U.S. District Court for the Northern District of California, "Case 1:16-mj-03168-BLG Document 1, Entered on FLSD Docket 08/30/2016," August 30, 2016, available at https://regmedia.co.uk/2016/09/02/linux_hack.pdf.

[3] Even such painstaking verification is likely to be ineffective against sophisticated adversaries.

requires knowing important details about how and when the compromise happened, which is not always possible.

Adkins then shared an example of a "perfect recovery," in which a small organization, after being breached in an espionage-related attack by a nation-state actor, removed and replaced all of its hardware, reinstalled all of its software, and verified all of its data by hand. The effort, although considered a successful example of high-assurance recovery, was enormously expensive and required shutting down the organization for a month. The example demonstrates that a "perfect recovery" is possible in certain contexts, when all the sources of the attack or breach are known and understood, but expensive and impractical in most scenarios.

Letting Go of Trust

Recovery is generally taken to mean returning systems to their normal, trustworthy state. However, Adkins posited that depending on trustworthiness in certain types of systems may be misplaced, and possibly unnecessary. With regard to Google's services, she said, employees work on what are called Zero-Trust networks. Adkins asked, if such a network were compromised, would it even matter? If you can remove the expectation of perfect trust in certain contexts, you can also remove the need for perfect recovery.

Further removing the emphasis on trust—for example, in hardware, operating systems, or other computing layers—could allow for a greater concentration of effort regarding trust and verification in the application and cryptographic code. In the context of applications, she noted that machine learning offers important avenues for audits, detection, and recovery. She argued that research into machine learning capabilities could, for example, lead to machine-assisted alteration-discovery systems capable of flagging suspicious code far more quickly than humans can. This could perhaps be used in breach recovery as a triage approach, by helping to concentrate code review efforts.

Enabling Recovery at Scale

Google is also reducing the emphasis on trusting personnel, such as SREs, in order to support operational reliability at scale. In practice, that means quickly building systems, recovering them, and migrating them when necessary, while also conducting regular, automated tests, including for catastrophic events. These practices are detailed in Google's book, *Site Reliability Engineering*.[4] It is also helpful to carefully consider metrics, to determine *what* exactly is useful to measure, Adkins said. For example, many organizations measure how often their backup processes complete successfully as a sign of a healthy business continuity program. She noted that Google, by contrast, looks

---

[4] B. Beyer, ed., *Site Reliability Engineering*, O'Reilly Media, Inc., Sebastopol, CA, 2016.

at how often the actual recovery of data (e.g., read off of tape) from backup media completes successfully.

Adkins noted that moving computing into the cloud, and away from end-user systems, can also help. Recent attacks like Spectre and Meltdown did not cause Google too many problems because the company had been able to seamlessly migrate customer workloads to patched systems.

Adkins pointed to a vulnerability in the Internet of Things (IoT) as another argument for machine-learning approaches. She noted that many of the millions of Internet-connected devices embed a program known as dnsmasq, which is maintained by independent developers instead of a large company. If one of those devices were to be hacked, it could be difficult to determine whether backdoors were added, or how many, or how they might affect devices using dnsmasq. She went on to observe that recovering from such a catastrophic breach could be made easier with alteration analysis, where code could be machine analyzed to detect changes or unwelcome additions at speeds far faster than humans could achieve.

An important report that influenced Adkins' security philosophy is James Anderson's 1972 *Computer Security Technology Planning Study* (known colloquially as "The Anderson Report"), in which Anderson asserts that computer security is not strong enough to prevent malicious events.[5] Adkins said that in a follow-up piece written a few years later, Anderson posited that the best way to improve security is to pair computer systems with humans via auditing and logging, practices that are still in use today.[6]

Looking at today's capabilities and the shifts that have occurred since the 1980s when the paradigm emphasizing reference monitors and a trusted computing base was established, Adkins proposed a new solution: teaching the machines not only to read logs and discover breaches, but to actually learn to defend themselves. While this solution may be still a long way off, Adkins pointed to recent encouraging examples, such as the 2016 Defense Advanced Research Projects Agency (DARPA) Cyber Grand Challenge, which proved that computers could be designed to defend themselves, and even counterattack.[7] Adkins also pointed out that by 2050, the scale of operations will make pairing humans and machines unfeasible. In addition, the scale of cyberspace will continue to grow. Right now it is global, but computers are already on Mars, and people may eventually be, too. She suggested that when computers can defend themselves, these automated defenses and counterattacks could usher in a new paradigm in which recovery is seen not as exceptional or catastrophic but simply as routine.

---

[5] J.P. Anderson, *Computer Security Technology Planning Study*, Volume 1, 1972, http://seclab.cs.ucdavis.edu/projects/history/papers/ande72a.pdf.

[6] J.P. Anderson, *Computer Security Threat Monitoring and Surveillance*, 1980, http://seclab.cs.ucdavis.edu/projects/history/papers/ande80.pdf.

[7] See the archived page for the Defense Advanced Research Projects Agency's Cyber Grand Challenge at http://archive.darpa.mil/cybergrandchallenge/.

Discussion

Adkins wrapped up with three main points. First, standards exist, but enforcing recovery practices solely through compliance to standards is impractical due to operational barriers. Second, we need to move toward automated detection and change the way we build trust in networks and systems. Finally, we need to teach machines to recover successfully themselves.

William Sanders, University of Illinois, Urbana-Champaign, asked if there were recovery practices that worked for both accidental failures and malicious attacks. Adkins said dual-use practices are ideal, but there are cases where this is not feasible. For example, an insider attacker with unknown motivation can pose a particularly significant and unique type of threat since the attacker could have high level capabilities such as system administrator privileges. Sanders also wondered if recovery practices were different depending on the security goal: If confidentiality were an issue, instead of availability, would the protocols be different? In response, Adkins noted that it is very difficult to tease out the borders between confidentiality and availability, which are both indicators of reliability.

Bob Blakley, Citigroup, noted that recovery can be extremely difficult, even when the root cause is not a malicious actor. For example, he pointed to the experience of a company that purchased security software that became corrupted and in turn corrupted some of the business systems it was supposed to protect. Recovery was arduous and took weeks. Building on this point, Peter Swire, Georgia Institute of Technology, asked if attacks perpetrated by nation-states fundamentally would require different recovery strategies than other attacks or accidental failures. Adkins replied that the recovery process is largely the same in most cases regardless of the root cause of the problem. SREs and security team members must work together to lessen the impact, determine the motivation, and act accordingly; while the playbook might be somewhat dynamic, the most important rubric is the end result—restoring a secure and functioning system.

Steven Lipner, SAFECode, pointed out that James Anderson believed that it was possible to eventually build a sufficiently strong system, although he recognized that there would still be the problem of holding people accountable for malicious insider attacks. Machine learning could help with accountability for malicious action by insiders, but the need in all cases is to determine what the bad actors did, and how long ago they did it.

Adkins replied that recovery requires forensic analysis with a focus on such questions as the following: What was the root cause? What did the attacker do? and Where did they go? It is very difficult to obtain all of that information, but usually a rough picture emerges. To do these analyses well today, they must be conducted manually and are time consuming, requiring a conservative approach in which every aspect of the system is assumed to be compromised. The day-to-day reality is that most companies are able to devote only limited resources to these issues—for example, paying for outside recovery services that operate for a limited time, meaning their search for data, story-building, and recovery could be rushed, and they would not get the whole story.

Paul Kocher, an independent researcher, noted that the number of places where data is stored is quickly growing, and he asked if that growth complicates the task of inventorying, analyzing, and restoring data. Adkins replied that at Google, infrastructure is relatively monolithic and centralized, and so despite the company's size, its operators have a fairly good handle on what is happening at all times. Outside of that specific context, though, Adkins said the answer is more complicated. For example, her own computer has more than 20 pieces of firmware, about which she knows virtually nothing, yet she must trust them to keep her data safe. Broadly speaking, she said, using devices from multiple manufacturers, with no standardization and an overreliance on trust, creates a situation that is nearly impossible to defend. But, she suggested increasing standardization and narrowing the realm of trust to the smallest area possible can offer a way forward.

RESILIENCE IN THE U.S. FINANCIAL SECTOR

David Edelman, Citigroup

David Edelman, a director at Citigroup with in-depth incident response experience dealing with large-scale financial systems, offered a unique perspective on how recoverability is viewed and handled in the financial sector.

Edelman explained that resilience is considered a top priority in the U.S. financial sector, both because banks and retail brokerages recognize its importance to their business and because government regulations require it. Rather than a static target or a far-off goal, he said resilience in the financial sector is a real, everyday requirement best thought of as a constant process with ever-changing adversaries.

A Shared System for Recoverability

Edelman noted that to be able to give customers an additional level of confidence in the ability of their banks to provide services even in the face of very sophisticated malicious activity, the financial industry created Sheltered Harbor.[8] While banks already capture every transaction every day within their own systems, Sheltered Harbor is an initiative undertaken by the sector as a whole that provides an additional layer of protection and enables rapid recovery and reconstitution of customer account status if needed.

---

[8] See the Sheltered Harbor website at http://www.shelteredharbor.org/.

Maintaining Data Confidentiality and Integrity

Edelman described how data confidentiality and integrity are central to Sheltered Harbor and other recoverability measures in the financial sector. The financial industry handles a huge volume of personally identifiable information. Sheltered Harbor employs sophisticated encryption and routine testing and verification to help ensure security. The system, he said, is built to be agile enough to use whatever is the most secure storage process available, whether that means publishing data onto tapes and storing it in a vault or—in the future—using a secure cloud-based system. If Sheltered Harbor were to move into the cloud, Edelman noted, the process would accommodate the necessary integrity verifications required before and after the encrypted data is uploaded. Edelman also noted that the processes and systems are designed so that data is easily auditable.

Discussion

Eric Grosse, an independent consultant, asked if a catastrophic event at one bank would actually affect all banks because money moves so frequently between them. Building on this point, Fred Schneider, Cornell University, asked whether the approach changes if a problem is not detected on the day it occurs but several days later. Edelman clarified that resetting a single bank's accounts to their state from the day before is a simple task that is inherent in most banks' business as usual processes and that pre-date Sheltered Harbor. In other failure scenarios, individual transactions can be reversed or restored based on when the problem occurred. He went on to explain that reversing transactions and restoring from archives from multiple days back is also possible, but in these cases, which are exceedingly rare, other banks can be affected, necessitating a wider recovery effort. Edelman noted that that process is the subject of many industry-wide exercises.

Bob Blakley, Citigroup, added that several additional processes also come into play in these more complex scenarios. For example, banks conduct daily clearances and settlements among themselves, so that their records are reconciled. This, combined with a typical 3-day settlement window for securities transactions, means that a bad event at one institution would not necessarily ripple across the entire industry.

William Sanders, University of Illinois, Urbana-Champaign, asked Edelman how often extreme recovery operations are needed. Edelman said that full recovery events are extremely rare. Even during the 2008 financial crisis, in which institutions were acquired by other institutions on very short notice, the acquiring institutions had access to the failed institutions' processing systems, data, and infrastructure.

RESILIENCE THE AMAZON WAY

Stephen Schmidt, Amazon Web Services

Stephen Schmidt, vice president of security engineering and chief information security officer at Amazon Web Services, led an open-ended session in which he invited workshop attendees to ask questions about Amazon's resilience practices. To frame the discussion, he opened by sharing Amazon's operational definition of resilience: "The ability of our customers to continue their business." In this context, he said, achieving resilience requires good technology, smart decisions, and an openness to constant learning.

Response to the 2017 S3 Outage

Bob Blakley, Citigroup, asked Schmidt to describe the steps taken after the Amazon S3 storage service outage, which lasted a few hours in February 2017. Schmidt first noted that one of his 2017 security goals, set before the outage, was to drastically reduce the number of humans with access to certain data, a deliberately difficult goal that would force an increased reliance on automation. This goal proved prescient, he observed, as the outage was the result of a typographical error by an authorized administrator executing approved commands.

He went on to explain that that single error led to a cascading failure, which propelled Amazon to make several changes. For example, he said, access and command execution at that level now require two-person authentication and authorization; in addition, commands that are most critical are now automated. Schmidt said that in order to figure out what those most critical commands are, Amazon used an existing internal security tool that maintains a record of commands executed by administrators of its internal systems; managers can use this tool to see exactly what actions employees are taking.

The security team was notified shortly after the outage began, Schmidt said. The response team first checked to see who was logged in to the affected area. Seeing approved users, they concluded that it was not a deliberate attack, and began manually analyzing the most recent commands executed. They identified the typo and started the recovery process. Because S3 is so large, recovery was complicated and involved several different service tiers.

The experience, Schmidt said, highlighted the importance of what he called good throttle design. Throttling (limiting the number of requests or changes to a system that can be submitted in a given timeframe) was a focus for improvement following the outage. Amazon has included throttling in its system APIs (application programming interfaces) for many years; however, in this case certain S3 subsystems did not have throttles in place. Changes following the outage included changes in capacity management tools, which enhanced safeguards to prevent large-scale capacity shifts that would bring subsystems below their minimum capacity levels.

The Role of the Cloud

Peter Swire, Georgia Institute of Technology, asked if Schmidt agreed with earlier speaker Heather Adkins, Google, Inc., that moving to the cloud improves prospects for recoverability. Schmidt said he agreed, adding that in his view there are very few workloads that would not work better in the cloud. Building on this, Swire wondered, if everything moves to the cloud, should we worry about a "monoculture" developing? Schmidt replied that monocultures in APIs should be considered differently from monocultures in the implementations underneath the APIs. Shared APIs provide a common interface format that allows for readily switching between services and moving workloads if needed. With respect to underlying implementations. there are other trade-offs to consider. Having only one version of a software stack becomes problematic if, for instance, a bug is found or introduced. Amazon keeps a small set of slightly different software versions on hand in case of such a problem, Schmidt said.

> Diversity of vendors reduces reliance on one specific vendor or product.

In terms of elements farther down in the stack, Schmidt added that Amazon, like many large companies, builds its own routers and switches, instead of relying on commercial products, to help ensure that the hardware works as expected and errors can be quickly caught. In fact, for items not created in-house, such as certain chips, the company intentionally uses a diversity of vendors to reduce reliance on one specific vendor or product, thus reducing their exposure if one becomes compromised.

In response to a question from Richard Danzig, Johns Hopkins University, Schmidt also pointed to the intelligence community's evaluation of Amazon's commercial cloud services (C2S), the results of which, he said, suggested that C2S engenders greater confidence than legacy data centers in terms of security. The root of C2S's strength, he explained, is its high level of visibility, meaning that changes are more easily auditable and made with more accountability than with more traditional architectures. He observed that this reflects a sea change in behavior and attitudes, away from the idea that a computer or system is "owned" because data is stored there, and toward an embrace of shared resources and cloud computing.

Lessons Learned

John Manferdelli, Northeastern University, asked what has surprised Schmidt in his experience. He answered that there have been both good surprises—for example, how resilient systems can be when human errors occur or how easy it has been to scale up well-built systems—and bad ones—for example, when naïve user or developer choices have led to bad situations.

At Amazon, he said, the goal is to break problems into small enough pieces such that teams can remain small and move quickly. To maintain connections and communication among these thousands of independent teams and projects, the principal engineering staff periodically review services and make changes or recommendations, he said. He noted that problems early in design cannot be easily undone, yet frequently cause headaches down the line. As a result, Schmidt said he has learned how crucial it is to involve his team in the process as early as possible.

He also emphasized the value of security teams being seen as partners instead of police or compliance officers. Beginning early to address security in partnership with the project team means his team can say yes to (reasonable) requests while minimizing risks, rather than merely swooping in and applying the brakes after a product is farther along in the pipeline. Steven Lipner, SAFECode, built on this point, noting that even if a "no" is required, saying it early enough in the process can lead to a better collaboration. Schmidt responded that rather than saying "no," he prefers for engineers to search for a clearer understanding of customer needs and then determine the best way to meet them.

Eric Grosse, an independent consultant, pointed to key lessons, such as the value of conducting forensics and the importance of keeping comprehensive logs, and asked Schmidt what additional practices he would consider useful industry-wide. Schmidt replied that backing up data is not as helpful as one might think, because backups inevitably decay and are not active portraits of your systems. Instead, he said, recovery systems should be built to be as active as possible. Fred Schneider, Cornell University, asked how Amazon could handle an attack that is not immediately detected if they have active backups, but not active replicas. Schmidt pointed to the importance of monitoring mechanisms and throttling as one important means to respond to anomalies. He added that it is also helpful to build systems with multiple components, or "shards," that can maintain system functionality while some components are inactive, which is, in a sense, a system of active replicas. Schmidt said that this system of active replicas that are constantly monitored was the most effective way they had found for cloud systems, although it might not be appropriate for every business case.

Resiliency in Practice

Susan Landau, Tufts University, asked Schmidt to expand on what Amazon means by resiliency and how that plays out in practice. Schmidt reiterated that Amazon sees its customer's needs as paramount, so resiliency for them means ensuring that their customers can do what they want to do when they want to do it, such as making sure that every API is responsive to customer requests. In the event of a problem, he said, Amazon will first try to contain it to prevent it from spreading further. The focus then turns to pinpointing exactly what went wrong and when, and finding alternate routes to deliver the data a customer needs. Once the shape of the problem becomes clear, he said, responders try to extrapolate what the hackers might do next, what they are capable of, and what problems have not been detected yet. The systems are returned to a safe starting point from before the attack, and an effort is made to remove the access doors the hackers used to get inside. Attribution (figuring out who is responsible for the problem), Schmidt said, is on the back burner during these steps, because knowing the individual responsible is generally not helpful for the recovery process.

Of course, Schmidt said, totally destroying the compromised system and building it back up from the ground would often be ideal, but that is not possible in every case or for every system component. When a customer has access to a cloud environment, the best course of action is to replace all the hardware involved. But other software components, such as a mySQL database, cannot be so easily disposed of and reconstituted.

Landau asked if the diverse needs of Amazon's customer base affects the company's resilience strategy. In terms of availability, Schmidt replied that Amazon is able to keep capacity fairly level across the board, so that a problem in one area does not usually affect availability in the other areas. In terms of customer priorities, Schmidt said Amazon recognizes that different customers have different requirements and preferences relevant to resiliency, and it builds and tests to those requirements. He also emphasized that the company takes regular, rigorous testing very seriously and said its operational teams are trained with frequent recovery drills.

Danzig asked how Amazon handles the unique security needs of one particular customer—the U.S. government—and whether the company's relationship with the government affects its resiliency practices. Schmidt said Amazon appreciates any intelligence it acquires that is specific and timely enough to be actionable. However, noting his own background in the Federal Bureau of Investigation before coming to Amazon, Schmidt said he understands that it can be challenging to strike the right balance between protecting hard-won intelligence and translating it into sharable, actionable information.

> It remains difficult to anticipate complex side-channel attacks in advance.

Scanning the Horizon

Manferdelli asked Schmidt to comment on promising new technologies or, on the flip side, inventive new types of threats that he anticipates in the future. Schmidt replied that breakthroughs in silicon involving instrumentation of certain behaviors in the silicon itself could be valuable for understanding processor use. As for future threats, Schmidt noted that it remains difficult to anticipate complex side-channel attacks in advance, although collecting more data on normal operations could help.

RESILIENCE AND RECOVERY IN THE ELECTRIC GRID

Timothy E. Roxey, North American Electric Reliability Corporation

Tim Roxey is the chief security officer and chief special operations officer for the North American Electric Reliability Corporation (NERC), a nonprofit international regulatory authority that works to assure the security and reliability of North America's bulk power system. He explored the challenges of identifying errors and deliberate attacks in the power grid's cyber infrastructure and the mechanisms used to provide continued service in the face of them.

Roxey said the average time between an attacker gaining access to an industrial control system component and an owner noticing the intrusion is 100 days—far longer than in some other industries such as military organizations or very sophisticated companies as discussed at the workshop. In some cases, he said, the intrusion can be discovered years later, or never discovered at all. In this context, the expectation in terms of recovery is not to get back to normal, but rather to create a "new normal" and adjust to it.

Roxey explained that in North America there are roughly 4,500 power companies serving about 365 million people running power through upwards of 58,000 substations. NERC runs a large-scale analytic program to identify intrusions across this vast network—24 hours a day, 7 days a week. On a daily basis, Roxey said, this program runs about 90 algorithms against several billion bytes of data collected each day and over 200 terabytes of data collected over the year. He said that this monitoring is done within a multi-layered framework for power grid cybersecurity and recovery whose key components include standards, maintenance, and information sharing.

Standards

The bottom, largest layer of the framework is the standards that govern how power systems meet various regulations, both online and in physical structures, to perform essential tasks. Because the electric grid is considered critical infrastructure, he noted, standards are explicitly designed and regulated to facilitate recovery, and companies are regularly audited to ensure compliance.

The regulatory component of NERC defines which providers and which aspects of the cyber infrastructure are critical infrastructure and oversees them accordingly. Roxey explained that roughly 2,000 of the 4,500 power companies fall into the category of requiring regulations, while the remaining 2,500 are considered sufficiently small or disconnected from each other that a security incident at one of them would not cause a cascading outage.

Standards are developed by using an open standards-setting process and many power companies are required to implement these standards. Roxey asserted that the power grid is the single most regulated sector, with regulations in this space ranging from personnel and training requirements to physical security perimeter requirements to recovery plans to vulnerability assessments, among many others. Although these are not best practices or guidelines, the regulations are enforceable, he emphasized. Because they are developed openly, however, attackers are well aware of them—as well as what they do not cover.

Maintenance

Another layer, maintenance, involves testing the system against potential threats in order to understand weaknesses and shore them up. Every 2 years, for example, NERC's GridEx exercises simulate a major grid challenge to which companies and government agencies attempt to respond. The lessons learned from these large-scale exercises can sometimes inspire new standards, but they always lead to better understandings, Roxey said, underscoring the industry's commitment to continuous improvement. Roxey encouraged participants to study and learn from the exercises, which are publicly available. He noted that the next exercise will encompass effects of a major outage on sectors such as water, communications, finance, and others, in recognition of the critical role of electricity in maintaining these sectors and our way of life.

Grid systems face numerous threats all the time. Roxey noted that electric system operators have been dealing with distributed denial of service (DDOS) attacks for nearly two decades, and in recent years, these attacks have reached astounding levels. In addition, he said, what are essentially accidental denial of service attacks can occur as a result of routine maintenance and upgrades—for example, when a network engineer attempts to use a new tool to scan a decades-old server that is unable to handle the load.

Such experiences underscore the need for advanced communication and preparation for routine operations, in addition to effective responses to deliberate attacks.

Apart from the systems supporting the financial sector, the electric grid is probably the most complex system on the planet, Roxey said. It is also regulated or influenced by an astounding number of organizations, such as the National Security Council, the Nuclear Industry Assessment Committee, the Electric Power Research Institute, the Federal Energy Regulatory Institute, and NERC itself, to name a few. He explained that each such organization has different concepts of resilience, recovery, and robustness, which are important to recognize and reconcile in order to create standards that satisfy many complex stakeholder needs.

Information Sharing

Discussing these needs and crafting regulations to meet them requires actionable information that can be shared. For example, cryptocurrency mining is a current challenge, but just naming the problem is not enough. To address it, information must be shared and it should be clear what cryptocurrency mining indicators are, so that companies know what to look for. Public-private collaboration for information sharing would improve security for everyone, Roxey said.

Discussion

Roxey concluded by reiterating the implications of the typically long lag time between when an intrusion occurs in the grid and when it is noticed. The bottom line is that there is a good chance that at any given time, there is an existing intrusion that has not yet been detected. Good regulations to support testing, detection capabilities, and incident response plans can help to minimize the fallout.

Peter Swire, Georgia Institute of Technology, asked if Roxey could explain why it has taken so long to restore power in Puerto Rico after Hurricane Maria. Roxey noted a number of factors that could be contributors to this problem, including the state of the infrastructure prior to the emergency, challenges in communications, and difficulties with logistics and access to affected areas.

William Sanders, University of Illinois, Urbana-Champaign, asked about enforcement of regulations. Roxey replied that audits can result in stiff fines. But perhaps more important, he said, is the establishment of a shared vocabulary in terms of compliance and protocols. In fact, problems today are found and reported much more often by companies themselves than by audits, a reversal from the situation just 10 years ago, he said, when penalties were far more common. Roxey said that compliance is a higher priority for companies today, and having common vocabulary and increased information sharing gives them the tools they need to comply.

COMMUNITY RESILIENCE AND THE FRAMEWORK FOR IMPROVING CRITICAL INFRASTRUCTURE FOR CYBERSECURITY

Stephen A. Cauffman and Matthew Barrett, National Institute of Standards and Technology

Stephen Cauffman and Matthew Barrett, both of the National Institute of Standards and Technology (NIST), offered a perspective on measuring community resilience and shared NIST's framework for improving critical infrastructure for cybersecurity.

Community Resilience

Cauffman, a research engineer in the Community Resilience Group (CRG),[9] began by noting that communities are complex "systems of systems" making them somewhat new territory for NIST's resilience work, which previously focused on individual buildings and their response to extreme events. By contrast, CRG focuses on the full recovery—social, economic, *and* infrastructural—of an entire community in the face of a natural or manmade disaster. In fact, Cauffman said, measuring the social and economic needs of a community after a disaster are essential to the process, because those needs drive the decisions and priorities relevant to creating more resilient buildings and infrastructure.

NIST is devoted to measurement science, but community resilience can be difficult to measure—a challenge compounded by the complexity of communities and all their dimensions. This lead CRG to devise a new, six-step process for assessing community resilience.

The first step is to reach out to community stakeholders, including elected officials, social and economic leaders, building owners, engineers, and architects. Second, those leaders work together to gain a wider understanding of a community's social dimensions, its built environment, and how the two are intertwined. Third, these stakeholders define their community's priorities, establish performance goals, and anticipate building performance in a disaster.

The final three steps are to evaluate gaps in building performance and identify solutions, finalize an official plan, and implement and maintain it. After a disaster, infrastructure is carefully assessed to determine how well it met recovery expectations, in both the short and long term. Gaps indicate where further improvements and solutions are needed. Together, these tangible steps link a community's physical infrastructure to its socioeconomic environment.

---

[9]NIST's Community Resilience Group conducts research and works with stakeholders to help improve community resilience for all hazards. They focus on the built environment, including infrastructure systems. Resilience efforts in other domains may provide useful lessons for recovery and resilience related to cybersecurity, communications, and information technology-related challenges.

NIST is strongly committed to this holistic, community-wide approach to disaster planning, Cauffman said. Although the impacts of disasters are often most visible in infrastructure, the social and economic consequences pose real challenges as well. Cauffman noted that Puerto Rico after Hurricane Maria is an unfortunate example. The island's poor infrastructure could not survive the storm, and that failure led to closed schools and health-care disruptions, exacerbating the damage to people's lives.

Cauffman explained that studying the socioeconomic impacts of compromised infrastructure on a community can lead to better solutions than assessing an area one building at a time. However, he said, right now, few tools exist to measure or model resilience holistically. The six-step process Cauffman described is only the first layer in creating decision-support tools to aid communities. NIST is also working on creating large-scale tools, in partnership with Colorado State University's Center for Risk-Based Community Resiliency Planning. By breaking down such a complex problem piece by piece, NIST hopes to create a framework for communities to be resilient and able to recover from disasters.

NIST Framework for Improving Critical Infrastructure for Cybersecurity

Barrett leads NIST's Framework for Improving Critical Infrastructure for Cybersecurity (the "Framework"). For the second half of the NIST presentation, Barrett explained the framework and its role in advancing resilience.

Cybersecurity is ultimately measured by outcomes, not procedures, Barrett stressed. Although individual companies may determine how much or how little security they need, NIST's role is to specify the level needed to enable resilience. The framework, he said, is not a list of rules but rather a decision-making tool for every company or community to think about how they will define and accomplish the five steps to creating cybersecurity: identify, protect, detect, respond, and recover. Although cybersecurity resilience is multidisciplinary and can be very complex, Cauffman said those five terms are valuable because they create a shared language for talking about resilience.

In response to a question from Mary Ellen Zurko, MIT Lincoln Laboratory, Barrett summarized the process used to develop the framework. His team started with a blank slate and was given 1 year to create a path to reducing the cybersecurity risk to critical infrastructure. Following the standard NIST model, the team openly engaged a variety of stakeholders, requested information and feedback, held workshops, and released a draft for public comment. This open dialogue and transparent process was instrumental in developing a framework that would be applicable across a variety of environments and work in most contexts, Barrett said.

The framework is currently being used to improve the overall regulatory ecosystem, including that for the electric sector, by making it more efficient and precise, Barrett said. Focusing on cybersecurity outcomes, not procedures, can ensure that everyone's goals are aligned. Building on the points raised earlier in the workshop with regard to the electric power sector, Barrett noted that compliance is a much more integral part of companies' operations today. Ensuring that regulations and the steps required to comply with them become ever more efficient and laser-focused on essential security can improve compliance as well as resilience and recovery, he suggested.

Weighing Resilience Investments and Trade-Offs

Kicking off the discussion, Bob Blakley, Citigroup, asked about the economic trade-offs involved in building in resilience strategies ahead of time versus paying for recovery after an event, and how the relative likelihood of different events in different communities weighs into that calculation. Cauffman stressed that mitigation—investing in resilience ahead of time—makes recovery faster, easier, and far more cost-efficient. In fact, he said, a recent report by the National Institute of Building Sciences showed that $1 in mitigation spending saves roughly $6 in future recovery expenses.[10] For events that are perhaps more rare or for events where recovery costs are lower, other strategies could include mutual aid partnerships, where organizations or regions pledge to help each other recover, such as by sending in crews to restring downed power lines. There are trade-offs to weigh in any case, and the community tools NIST is developing include an economic component to help stakeholders assign an actual dollar value to their options.

Cauffman also suggested realigning how we think about the "resilience curve" to better reflect the real-world trajectories of communities after disasters. The resilience curve is traditionally conceived as a straight line that dips down when an event occurs and then gradually returns to the starting state. In reality, Cauffman said, communities are most often starting out on either an upward or downward trajectory, and that initial trajectory affects what happens after the event. A community on the upswing, for example, is more likely to bounce back quickly and can sometimes even rebuild itself in ways that make it stronger and more resilient after the event. But communities already in decline will be much worse off after a disaster, and are unlikely to get back to the way they were before the event.

Cauffman pointed to New Orleans' experience after Hurricane Katrina as a mix of these two extremes; while the city has never recovered its original state, and many residents moved away permanently, the rebuilding effort attracted heavy investment, creating a revitalized New Orleans that is very different from the city that existed before the storm.

---

[10]National Institute of Building Sciences, "National Institute of Building Sciences Issues New Report on the Value of Mitigation," press release, January 11, 2018, http://www.nibs.org/news/381874/National-Institute-of-Building-Sciences-Issues-New-Report-on-the-Value-of-Mitigation.htm.

Barrett added that the NIST framework enables users to define and balance the "before" (identify, protect) and "after" (detect, respond, recover) periods of a disaster to inform a resource investment strategy.

Defining Communities and Dealing with Interdependencies

Noting that communities are complex, interconnected, interdependent systems, Tadayoshi Kohno, University of Washington, asked how those interdependencies affect the way we assess capacity for recovery and resilience. Is it possible to ensure that assumptions about multiple, interconnected communities are satisfied all at the same time?

Cauffman answered that NIST defines communities by geographic boundaries and the presence of a local governance structure. Local, state, and federal government jurisdictions often overlap, and infrastructures can be regional, but constraining the focus by geography and governance helps to break the resilience challenge into logical and manageable pieces. Electricity may come from far away, and hospitals may be administered by external stakeholders, but the six-step process should, by and large, create an avenue to address those interdependencies and ensure assumptions are accurate, he said.

> It is difficult to strike the right balance in identifying essential services without creating more dependencies.

Fred Schneider, Cornell University, noted that this "divide and conquer" strategy can be a successful solution to difficult problems. It is logical to divide things geographically (akin to taking a building-by-building approach, but on a larger scale) or by sector (e.g., looking at power grid resiliency specifically). However, he said, interdependency is a different type of layer that makes the problem significantly more tricky. If roads are blocked, it can be hard to restore power. If power is out, it makes communication difficult. This close coupling of resources creates dependencies. Dependencies are logically built into cyber systems; one cannot bring up the database before the storage server is in place. He asked how we can account for such relationships in recovery planning.

To this point, Barrett pointed to two relevant concepts: essential services and secure engineering. One way of approaching dependencies in the physical world, he said, is by defining essential services and using secure engineering to build them with resilience factors in place. But it can be tricky to strike the right balance in identifying essential services without creating ever more dependencies. The classical computer science concept of common controls, in which many controls are handled by a few pieces, is meant to increase efficiency, but can have the effect of increasing dependencies and potentially undermining resiliency. This conundrum is analogous to essential services in a community.

Opportunities in the Internet of Things

Noting that much of the discussion had focused on designing resiliency into systems and communities, Kohno asked about the role that commercial, off-the-shelf products could potentially play in resilience and recovery strategies. For example, IoT devices could potentially be used to determine when a community is in a state of emergency and divert power away from nonessential services.

Cauffman replied that there is potential for IoT devices to help, especially as technological capabilities grow and costs decline. For example, he pointed to the availability of low-cost smart flood gauges that provide real-time water level data to communities to inform decision making and help move people out of harm's way. However, he underscored that in most communities resilience challenges are still incompletely defined, and at this stage it is important to focus on more fully understanding the problems before shifting our focus to developing technological solutions to address them.

3

Closing Observations and Discussion

CLOSING OBSERVATIONS

Richard J. Danzig, Johns Hopkins University

Richard Danzig, Johns Hopkins University, wrapped up the workshop with a summary of observations and then moderated an open discussion among forum members, speakers, and workshop attendees.

Danzig pointed to two distinct dimensions in the arena of recoverability: the human and the technological. Although we often focus on the technological problems and solutions, the human dimension affects both system requirements and system performance, he said. He went on to note that recovery and resilience are as much psychological and social issues as they are technical ones.

We are in the early stages of fully grasping what cyber recovery and resiliency means, he continued, and our psychological expectations of what is acceptable and unacceptable will change over time. If, when cars were first invented, we knew they would eventually cause 35,000 deaths yearly, their adoption might have taken a different trajectory, he said. Danzig observed that we are now psychologically used to cars and their consequences now and we accept those risks daily, while we remain uncomfortable with the risks of cybersecurity breaches.

Predicting future risks and attitudes toward them is difficult. Just a few years ago, Danzig said, some underestimated the impact of Internet of Things (IoT) devices and how vulnerable IoT users would be to bad actors. And, he emphasized, it is ultimately users, and not the technology itself, who are the targets of attacks and who suffer their fallout. When Sony was hacked in 2014, business was disrupted, but he argued that the greatest pain came from the public exposure of private thoughts. Similarly, Russian interference in the 2016 election targeted voters, not voting machines.

Danzig suggested directing more attention to determining what is an acceptable length of time between an attack and its detection and recovery, a timeline that varies substantially across sectors and environments and depends on the nature of the vulnerabilities as well as potential damages from attacks. In some contexts, it may be acceptable if it takes a long time to discover a problem or if a system has to be shut down for a month to recover, but in other contexts, such as elections, stock markets, or war, such delays could be catastrophic psychologically and socially. Here again, the importance of time is tied to the human dimensions of disruptions, not the technological ones.

> Frequent exposure to resilience and recovery processes can improve adaptation prospects.

Danzig observed that frequent exposure to resilience and recovery processes can lead to an environment in which problems are adapted to as a matter of course. If resiliency were better incorporated into our day-to-day landscape, Danzig suggested, the costs to design and maintain it would become a familiar and justifiable expense, perhaps akin to national vaccination programs.

Industries and communities can improve resilience and recovery by prioritizing frequent training, both before and after security incidents, Danzig argued. Instead of trying to hide or move past those situations, we should be sharing information, learning from mistakes, and improving procedures. Danzig recommended *Antifragile* by Nassim Nicholas Taleb to participants, which argues that the goal of resilience isn't to get you back to where you were, but to teach you how to rebuild to become better than before.[1]

Addressing the technological dimension, Danzig noted that while machines do have vulnerabilities, we should keep in mind that they also possess extraordinary abilities that can be used to promote resilience and recovery. For example, every keystroke can be documented and used to bolster deterrence, attribution, and retribution practices. Machine learning and artificial intelligence (AI) capabilities could also be harnessed to tackle the challenges of complex systems, many of which are beyond individual human capabilities, he suggested.

---

[1] N.N. Taleb, *Antifragile*, Penguin Books, Ltd., New York, 2012.

Danzig argued that the growth of the cloud is also promising for security, resilience, and recovery. Startups no longer need to create their own security systems, he observed, but can increasingly rely on expertly created ones. This may create a monoculture, but, Danzig added, it also provides a level of security, visibility, and technical sophistication that would otherwise not be available to smaller companies.

Danzig concluded by reminding attendees that the future, and its challenges, are still unknown to us, but the way that we design tools matters. The increased adoption of artificial intelligence, IoT, and virtual reality systems suggests that it is increasingly important that those systems be "antifragile" by design. Computing power and sophistication might be increasing exponentially along some dimensions, but human capabilities are not.

CLOSING PLENARY DISCUSSION

The workshop ended with an open discussion covering many topics, including the importance of learning from the past, understanding time and scale in different contexts, and sharing information. Many participants reiterated Danzig's suggestion that the focus in security and resilience should shift from trying to predict the future and preventing problems from occurring and toward making resilience and the ability to recover a part of the everyday landscape across all sectors.

Learning from the Past

Several participants discussed past events that contain lessons for recovery. Susan Landau, Tufts University, shared two examples that illustrate how varied the challenges can be. A 2008 distributed denial of service attack on the country of Georgia created an atmosphere of misinformation and chaos that Russia was able to take advantage of. Russia's interference techniques have been particularly challenging, she added, because they target humans, not just systems and infrastructure. On the other hand, she said, other examples illustrate how resilient human beings can be. Vermont is a state subjected to far more snowstorms than hurricanes. When Hurricane Irene pummeled the state in 2011, the people proved more resilient than the infrastructure. The hurricane washed away fifteen bridges, and it took years to rebuild them all, while the communities, finding themselves isolated for days or weeks in the immediate aftermath, managed the situation admirably.

Tim Roxey, North American Electric Reliability Corporation (NERC), talked about learning from the August 2003 blackout, when the power grid shut off in much of the Northeastern United States. NERC has implemented several new standards since that incident, including vegetation maintenance and better emergency communication between stations and operators.

Steven Lipner, SAFECode, noted that James Anderson's 1972 report, mentioned by Adkins, actually sent computer science researchers down an ultimately unproductive path for decades. Zurko agreed, noting that we can learn from that failure and apply it to today's expectations of users and recovery. Lipner added that learning from experience is an essential piece of this process. Root cause analyses are extremely important, but they are only helpful if they lead to changes that prevent future problems. He also stressed the importance of respecting the limits to how much we can "engineer" users.

Experimentation and learning from mistakes can help craft guiding principles.

Lampson shared an example of another past failure that contains an important lesson. More than 20 years ago, NIST issued password-creation recommendations, and Lampson recently learned that they were created by an employee who didn't have the right level of user experience expertise. Two important elements were ignored: the root cause of the problem and user limitations. The unintended result was the creation of countless easy-to-steal passwords.

Peter Swire, Georgia Institute of Technology, noted that the Army constantly studies past battles. John Manferdelli, Northeastern University, agreed that learning from the past is important, but forward progress is also essential. The Army has to fight the current war, not just implement ideas that might have helped in the last one. It's also important to remember how experimentation and learning from mistakes can help craft guiding principles, he continued, something that, for example, has helped the nuclear submarine community improve overall reliability.

Considering Time and Scale

Bob Blakley, Citigroup, reiterated Danzig's point that time is a crucial consideration for framing recoverability. In the financial sector, in addition to the end-of-day rule which requires that accounts are settled at the close of every business day, banks may also be placed into receivership by regulators if they are unable to conduct business operations for a number of consecutive days. These time limits help identify and shape critical recovery procedures in the industry.

Building on this, Swire added that time and scale vary greatly in different contexts, and recovery discussions must include these definitions in order to determine the best course of action. Time could mean weeks or milliseconds. Scale can be equally varied.

Recoverability as a First-Class Security Objective

Blakley agreed, and noted that most large banks practice recovery procedures at various scales including the level of the application, machine, data center, national subsidiary, and entire firm.

Eric Grosse, independent consultant, expressed surprise that there can be lags of 100 days or more in between attack and detection in some sectors and environments. In his experience at a major web services company, failures are detected within minutes and systems are expected to recover within minutes of detection. An event that could persist for weeks or months would be incredibly rare, he said.

Danzig asked Roxey how long it would take to bring up a large power grid in the event of a cyberattack. Roxey replied that it depends on how large the attack and the grid are, but generally speaking, it would take somewhere between a few hours to a few days. An important question, Roxey noted, is not only whether the power is back on, but whether hackers are able to cause damage to the system.

Danzig noted another nuance affecting timelines, which is that most resilience practices were born out of situations with time and space limitations that do not neatly translate into the types of cyberattacks we must contend with today. It is obvious when a hurricane is over or a building has fallen, he said, but it is less obvious when a cyberattack is over. In many cases there is a chance that the attacker has merely changed course and will continue to be able to attack a different area.

Information Sharing

Lipner expanded on the idea of information sharing, an issue raised by several presenters. The government does share information with industry, but commercial companies may not always see the benefit of passing their own information along. Blakley said that in his experience, there can be effective, mutual information sharing between government and industry, noting that financial institutions have received actionable information from the government.

Danzig cautioned that informal information bartering within industry tends to benefit the largest companies in a field, while the smaller ones can be shut out of the relationship. The quality of the information, regardless of whether it is shared with other companies or the government, is also important, he stressed.

Responding, Grosse pointed out that smaller companies can still be a part of the information sharing. Even if they do not have information to offer, he said, they are allowed to participate if they can be trusted not to leak. Landau added that different industries may have different conceptions of what information is considered helpful and actionable.

Day-to-Day Resilience

Lipner reiterated Danzig's suggestion that resilience strategies must be practiced and deployed frequently to be effective. Over his years in the field, he said he has learned that it is crucial not only to make recovery plans, but also to enact and practice them frequently so they become routine and companies are in a state of readiness. Manferdelli agreed that practice is important, but it first requires data, which in turn requires funding, something that may be in short supply at different times in an organization's lifespan. In addition, the challenges are further compounded by the fact that computing conditions are constantly changing, technology is not always transparent, and scale varies greatly. We are still getting used to the complications of a computing world, he said, much in the way that it took decades to get used to the benefits and drawbacks of the automotive world. In response to a question from Danzig, Manferdelli said that recovery discussions should balance inductive and deductive reasoning, but there is currently a lack of theory development and deduction, pointing to a need for more principle-based solutions, in addition to more data.

Tadayoshi Kohno, University of Washington, pointed out that there are resilience needs that go beyond critical infrastructure and national security. In the future, products and industries we cannot even imagine will have security and recovery needs, and he suggested a need to broaden recovery planning to cast a wider net.

Paul Kocher, independent researcher, noted that while resiliency is a key focus and recovery is working well in some areas, such as cloud attacks, there is a much larger area of technology where resiliency planning is not happening, such as cooling systems within computers. These aspects are more mundane, but still require attention, he argued. He speculated that there are probably not that many engineers today who could patch and stabilize a computer chip designed 12 years ago. Such planning is a complex problem that needs to be simplified first, he continued, especially as the number of electronic devices grows but it remains difficult and expensive to make sure they can continue to be updated.

Looking Toward the Future

Participants discussed several additional resources that are useful in thinking about resilience and recovery going forward. Blakley and Danzig pointed to Dan Geer's keynote[2] from Source Boston 2017, in which Geer argued that the fate of the future will be decided by the actions security technologists take now. Landau offered two recommendations for how to think about the future and the human element: she

---

[2] See D. Geer, "SOURCE Boston, Closing Keynote," nominal delivery draft, April 27, 2017, http://geer.tinho.net/geer.source.27iv17.txt.

reminded the audience of the 1999 paper "Users are not the enemy,"[3] and mentioned Duo, a security platform that in her view incorporates the human dimension well.

Fred Schneider, Cornell University, noted that previous forum workshops had focused on different recovery aspects, including identity theft[4] and cryptographic agility,[5] and suggested that integrating the present discussion with those previous ones could help achieve a more complete view of the problem. At Danzig's request, Schneider also spoke about "graceful degradation," the ability of a machine to continue functioning even if a large part of it has been compromised. As more sectors leverage artificial intelligence (AI) to increase efficiency and effectiveness, graceful degradation should be considered in that context, as well. He argued that too many new devices and technologies are built with AI but without careful recovery planning and are degrading ungracefully. Butler Lampson, Microsoft Research, pointed out that not all systems need to degrade gracefully. Schneider agreed, but noted that there is an important difference between considering and then discarding such a goal and never considering it at all, which he believes to be the case in the context of many emerging technologies.

Blakley raised an additional concern about AI, the notion that reliance on AI can de-skill the workforce to the point that if the AI breaks, not only is staff unable to fix it, they cannot even complete the tasks themselves in order to keep serving customers. Landau agreed that resiliency planning and AI in the workforce need to be examined carefully, and also suggested that considering computers as disposable elements could improve our ability to maintain updated software and reduce the temptation to invest undue trust in any one component.

> As more sectors leverage AI, graceful degradation will be important to consider in that context.

Closing Discussion

Closing out the workshop, Danzig reiterated that recovery is a balancing act. We can argue for more investment in resilience, more graceful degradation, and better security, but these also incur substantial costs that can drag down innovation. There is also the chance that we could over-invest in pursuing the wrong ideas.

---

[3] A. Adams and M.A. Sasse, Users are not the enemy, *Communications of the ACM* 42(12):40-46, 1999.

[4] See National Academies of Sciences, Engineering, and Medicine, *Data Breach Aftermath and Recovery for Individuals and Institutions: Proceedings of a Workshop*, The National Academies Press, Washington, DC, 2016, https://doi.org/10.17226/23559.

[5] See National Academies of Sciences, Engineering, and Medicine, *Cryptographic Agility and Interoperability: Proceedings of a Workshop*, The National Academies Press, Washington, DC, 2017, https://doi.org/10.17226/24636.

When writing was invented, Danzig noted, the Greeks worried that it would ruin people's ability to memorize things. It did, but it also brought unforeseen benefits that eventually outweighed the disadvantages. We are still in the early stages of thinking about recovery, and unfortunately the early years are the hardest. Eventually, good strategies will be adopted, he observed, but it may take many years, and many attacks, to understand what the real solutions are, a trajectory similar to that of aviation, which progressed from a daring and dangerous pursuit to a safe, routine means of transportation.

A good solution, he emphasized, will require acknowledging that different industries have very different priorities and resources. In the financial world, the assets are digital and banks have the funds to secure them, Danzig suggested. In the electric sector, the assets are physical and security is less heavily resourced. Finding the right solution, he noted, will also take experimentation, investment, and learning from inevitable attacks and mistakes.

Appendixes

A Workshop Agenda and Participants List

WORKSHOP ON RECOVERABILITY AS A FIRST-CLASS SECURITY OBJECTIVE

February 8, 2018
Keck Center of the National Academies of Sciences, Engineering, and Medicine
Washington, D.C.

AGENDA

12:30 p.m.	Welcome and Overview Fred B. Schneider, Forum Chair
12:35	Framing Keynote Butler W. Lampson, Microsoft Research
1:25	Heather Adkins, Google, Inc.
2:15	David Edelman, Citigroup
3:00	Break
3:15	Stephen Schmidt, Amazon
4:00	Timothy E. Roxey, North American Electric Reliability Corporation
4:45	Stephen Cauffman and Matthew Barrett, National Institute of Standards and Technology
5:30	Wrap-up Discussion, Reactions, and Continued Q&A Richard Danzig, Moderator
6:00	Adjourn Workshop

Reception for Members, Speakers, and Attendees

PARTICIPANTS LIST

Heather Adkins, Google, Inc.
Anita L. Allen, University of Pennsylvania
Robert Axelrod, University of Michigan
Matthew Barrett, National Institute of Standards and Technology
Paul Beaton, National Academies of Sciences, Engineering, and Medicine
Cherrie Black, Idaho National Laboratory
Bob Blakley, Citigroup
Travis Breaux
Yousaf Butt, U.S. Department of State
Fred Cate, Indiana University
Lonnie Carey, Jr., Office of the Director of National Intelligence
Stephen Cauffman, National Institute of Standards and Technology
Fred Chang, Southern Methodist University
Dean Checknita, National Protection and Programs Directorate, Department of Homeland Security
Steve Crocker, Shinkuro, Inc.
Richard J. Danzig, Johns Hopkins University Applied Physics Laboratory
Antonio DeSimone, Johns Hopkins University Applied Physics Laboratory
Donna Dodson, National Institute of Standards and Technology
Ann Drobnis, Computing Community Consortium
David Edelman, Citigroup
Eric Grosse, Independent Consultant
David Hoffman, Intel Corporation
Bonnie Hong, Idaho National Laboratory
Paul Kocher, Independent Researcher
Tadayoshi Kohno, University of Washington
Jim Kurose, National Science Foundation
Butler W. Lampson, Microsoft Research
Susan Landau, Tufts University
Carl Landwehr, George Washington University
Steven Lipner, SAFECode
John Manferdelli, Northeastern University
Brad Martin, National Security Agency
Kevin Reifsteck, National Security Council
Timothy E. Roxey, North American Electric Reliability Corporation
William Sanders, University of Illinois, Urbana-Champaign
Fred B. Schneider, Cornell University
Stephen Schmidt, Amazon
Alan Shaw, National Academies of Sciences, Engineering, and Medicine
Kay Smith, Massachusetts Institute of Technology Alumni / Organization of the Petroleum Exporting Countries
Peter Swire, Georgia Institute of Technology
David Vladeck, Georgetown University Law Center
Mary Ellen Zurko, Massachusetts Institute of Technology Lincoln Laboratory

B | Steering Committee Biographies

FRED B. SCHNEIDER is the Samuel B. Eckert Professor of Computer Science at Cornell University and chair of the department. He joined Cornell's faculty in fall 1978, having completed a Ph.D. at Stony Brook University and a B.S. in engineering at Cornell in 1975. Schneider's research has always concerned various aspects of trustworthy systems—systems that will perform as expected, despite failures and attacks. Most recently, his interests have focused on system security. His work characterizing what policies can be enforced with various classes of defenses is widely cited, and it is seen as advancing the nascent science base for security. He is also engaged in research concerning legal and economic measures for improving system trustworthiness. Schneider was elected a fellow of the American Association for the Advancement of Science (AAAS, 1992), the Association of Computing Machinery (ACM, 1995), and the Institute of Electrical and Electronics Engineers (IEEE, 2008). He was named professor-at-large at the University of Tromso (Norway) in 1996 and was awarded a doctor of science honoris causa by the University of Newcastle-upon-Tyne in 2003 for his work in computer dependability and security. He received the 2012 IEEE Emanuel R. Piore Award for "contributions to trustworthy computing through novel approaches to security, fault-tolerance, and formal methods for concurrent and distributed systems." The National Academy of Engineering (NAE) elected Schneider to membership in 2011, and the Norges Tekniske Vitenskapsakademi (Norwegian Academy of Technological Sciences) named him a foreign member in 2010. He is currently a member of the Naval Studies Board and the Computer Science and Telecommunications Board of the National Academies of Sciences, Engineering, and Medicine, and is founding chair of the National Academies' Forum on Cyber Resilience.

ANITA L. ALLEN is the Henry R. Silverman Professor of Law and Professor of Philosophy at the University of Pennsylvania Law School, where she is also the university's vice provost for faculty. She is an expert on privacy law, bioethics, and contemporary values, and is recognized for her scholarship about legal philosophy, women's rights, and race relations. In 2010 she was appointed by President Obama to the Presidential Commission for the Study of Bioethical Issues. Her books include *Unpopular Privacy: What Must We Hide* (2011); *Privacy Law and Society* (2011); *The New Ethics: A Guided Tour of the 21st Century Moral Landscape* (2004); *Why Privacy Isn't Everything: Feminist Reflections on*

Personal Accountability (2003); and *Uneasy Access: Privacy for Women in a Free Society* (1988). She co-edited (with Milton Regan) *Debating Democracy's Discontent* (1998). Allen, who has written more than a 100 scholarly articles, has also contributed to popular magazines and blogs and has frequently appeared on nationally broadcast television and radio programs. She has served on numerous editorial and advisory boards and on the boards of a number of local and national nonprofits and professional associations, including the Hastings Center, the Electronic Information Privacy Center, and the Bazelon Center for Mental Health Law.

ERIC GROSSE is a senior member of the Google security team and was previously vice president, Security & Privacy Engineering, at Google in Mountain View, California, leading a team of 512 who ensure systems and data stay safe and users' privacy remains secure. Improved and wider use of SSL, stronger consumer authentication technology, detection and blocking of espionage, transparency on legal requests for data, sophisticated malware analysis, tools and frameworks for safer building of Web applications are among the achievements of the Google Security Team. Before Google, Grosse was a research director and fellow at Lucent Bell Labs where he worked on security, networking, algorithms for approximation and visualization, software distribution, and scientific computing. He has a Ph.D. in computer science from Stanford University.

BUTLER W. LAMPSON is a technical fellow at Microsoft Corporation and an adjunct professor at the Massachusetts Institute of Technology (MIT). He has worked on computer architecture, local area networks, raster printers, page description languages, operating systems, remote procedure call, programming languages and their semantics, programming in the large, fault-tolerant computing, transaction processing, computer security, WYSIWYG editors, and tablet computers. He was one of the designers of the SDS 940 time-sharing system, the Alto personal distributed computing system, the Xerox 9700 laser printer, two-phase commit protocols, the Autonet LAN, the SPKI system for network security, the Microsoft Tablet PC software, the Microsoft Palladium high-assurance stack, and several programming languages. He received the ACM Software Systems Award in 1984 for his work on the Alto, the IEEE Computer Pioneer award in 1996, the von Neumann Medal in 2001, the Turing Award in 1992, and the NAE's Draper Prize in 2004. He is a member of the National Academy of Sciences and the NAE and a fellow of the ACM and the American Academy of Arts and Sciences.

SUSAN LANDAU is a professor of cybersecurity policy in the Department of Social Science and Policy Studies at Worcester Polytechnic Institute. Landau has been a senior staff privacy analyst at Google, a Distinguished Engineer at Sun Microsystems, a faculty member at the University of Massachusetts, Amherst, and at Wesleyan University. She has held visiting positions at Harvard, Cornell, Yale, and the Mathematical Sciences Research Institute. Landau is the author of *Surveillance or Security? The Risks Posed by New Wiretapping Technologies* (2011) and co-author, with Whitfield Diffie, of *Privacy on the Line: The Politics of Wiretapping and Encryption* (1998, rev. ed. 2007). She has written numerous computer science and public policy papers and op-eds on cybersecurity and encryption policy and testified to Congress on the security risks of wiretapping and on cybersecurity activities at National Institute of Standards and Technology's Information Technology Laboratory. Landau currently serves on the Computer Science Telecommunications Board of the National Academies. A 2012 Guggenheim fellow, Landau was a 2010–2011 fellow at the Radcliffe Institute for Advanced Study, the recipient of the 2008 Women of Vision Social Impact Award, and a fellow of the AAAS and the ACM. She received her B.A. from Princeton University, her M.S. from Cornell University, and her Ph.D. from MIT.

Speaker Biographies

HEATHER ADKINS is a 15-year Google veteran and founding member of the Google Security Team. As director of information security, she has built a global team responsible for maintaining the safety and security of Google's networks, systems, and applications. She has an extensive background in systems and network administration with an emphasis on practical security and has worked to build and secure some of the world's largest infrastructure. She now focuses her time primarily on the defense of Google's computing infrastructure and working with industry to tackle some of the greatest security challenges as part of the Defending Digital Democracy project at the Belfer Center for Science and International Affairs at Harvard Kennedy School.

MATTHEW BARRETT leads Cybersecurity Framework activities at the National Institute of Standards and Technology (NIST). Barrett and his team are responsible for establishing and maintaining relationships with both private and public sector (Cybersecurity) Framework stakeholders. Barrett works through those relationships to provide perspective and guidance, as well as gather input on use and evolution of the Framework. To fulfill stakeholder needs, he also collaborates with a variety of NIST cybersecurity programs. Barrett is known for his leadership of NIST's Security Content Automation Protocol program and support of the Office and Management and Budget's Federal Desktop Core Configuration initiative (predecessor to U.S. Government Consensus Baseline). Previous to NIST and over the past decade, he served in various executive roles including roles such as president and chief executive officer.

STEPHEN CAUFFMAN is a research engineer with the Community Resilience Program at NIST. He initiated resilience work at NIST in 2011 with funding from the Department of Homeland Security and developed the initial plan for the NIST Community Resilience Program. The program is developing science-based tools to measure resilience at the community-scale and produced the Community Resilience Planning Guide for Buildings and Infrastructure Systems and the Community Resilience Economic Decision Support Guide for Buildings and Infrastructure Systems (https://www.nist.gov/topics/community-resilience). The program is supported by the NIST-funded Center for Risk-Based Community Resilience Planning, a ten-institution team led by Colorado State University (http://resilience.colostate.edu/). Cauffman served as the program manager for the World Trade Center Investigation, led NIST's study of the performance of structures following Hurricanes Katrina and Rita, and was a member of the team that studied the collapse of the Dallas Cowboys Practice Facility. He has served as leader of the Structures Group and as deputy chief and acting chief of the Materials and Structural Systems Division.

RICHARD J. DANZIG is vice chair of the board of trustees of the RAND Corporation, a member of the Defense Policy Board and the President's Intelligence Advisory Board, a trustee of Reed College, a director of the Center for a New American Security, and a director of Saffron Hill Ventures (a European investment firm). Recently he has been a director of National Semiconductor Corporation and Human Genome Sciences Corporation. He has also served as chairman of the board of the Center for a New American Security and chairman of the board of the Center for Strategic and Budgetary Assessments. From the spring of 2007 through the Presidential election of 2008, Danzig was a senior advisor to Senator Obama on national security issues. Danzig served as the 71st Secretary of the Navy from November 1998 to January 2001. He was the Under Secretary of the Navy between 1993 and 1997. Danzig is a member of the Aspen Strategy Group and a senior advisor at the Center for New American Security, the Center for Naval Analyses, and the Center for Strategic and International Studies in Washington, D.C. His primary activity is as a consultant to the Departments of Defense and Homeland Security on terrorism.

DAVID EDELMAN is a director at Citigroup where he has worked for the past 25 years currently holding the title of chief cyber security scientist. Over this period of time, he has held positions in operations, architecture, continuity of business, and information security in locations in the United States and Europe. As an internal entrepreneur, he has created and developed a number of organizations subsequently handing them over to business as usual operations. He is one of the architects of Citigroup's Internet presence and is the architect of Citigroup's network component security. He is actively involved in the Financial Services Sector Coordinating Council (FSSCC), the Financial Services-Information Sharing and Analysis Center (FS-ISAC), and the Sheltered Harbor Technology and Security Architecture work stream. He serves as the co-chair of the FS-ISAC's Cyber Agility Task Force. Edelman is a long time member of the IEEE and the ACM.

BUTLER W. LAMPSON is a technical fellow at Microsoft Corporation and an adjunct professor at MIT. He has worked on computer architecture, local area networks, raster printers, page description languages, operating systems, remote procedure call, programming languages and their semantics, programming in the large, fault-tolerant computing, transaction processing, computer security, WYSIWYG editors, and tablet computers. He was one of the designers of the SDS 940 time-sharing system, the Alto personal distributed computing system, the Xerox 9700 laser printer, two-phase commit protocols, the Autonet LAN, the SPKI system for network security, the Microsoft Tablet PC software, the Microsoft Palladium high-assurance stack, and several programming languages. He received the ACM Software Systems Award in 1984 for his work on the Alto, the IEEE Computer Pioneer award in 1996 and von Neumann Medal in 2001, the Turing Award in 1992, and the NAE's Draper Prize in 2004. He is a member of the National Academy of Sciences and the National Academy of Engineering and a fellow of the ACM and the American Academy of Arts and Sciences.

TIMOTHY E. ROXEY is vice president and chief E-ISAC operations officer of the North American Electric Reliability Corporation (NERC). He is responsible for development and execution of key critical infrastructure protection initiatives, such as NERC's cybersecurity risk preparedness assessment and other continuous risk assessment efforts. Roxey also acts as a key coordination point for North American government officials and is a member of the Electricity Sector Information Sharing and Analysis Center (ES-ISAC) activities. He has 30 years of experience in the nuclear utility industry serving in organizations such as operations, information technology, licensing, and security, among others. Roxey has over 35 years of computer-related experience working in environments from mainframes, minis, and micros to hand-wired special control systems. He has written numerous programs in many different languages. Roxey is a widely recognized leader in the fields of security and infrastructure protection, formerly serving as deputy chair of the Nuclear Sector Coordinating Council and chairman of its Cyber Security Sub-Council. He is presently the private sector chairman of the Industrial Controls System Joint Working Group. Roxey spent over 17 years with Constellation Energy. At Constellation, he was the technical assistant to the vice chairman for security related matters and was involved in a variety of both physical and cybersecurity issues across the entire nuclear sector of the United States. In the realm of physical security, Roxey was involved in reviewing security system architectures for the next generation of nuclear power in America as a member of the various oversight committees. He also served, by invitation, on two presidential commissions helping to prepare guidance for the next administration.

STEPHEN SCHMIDT is vice president & chief information security officer for Amazon Web Services (AWS). His duties at AWS include leading product design, management, and engineering development efforts focused on bringing the competitive, economic, and security benefits of cloud computing to business and government customers. Prior to joining AWS, Schmidt had an extensive career at the Federal Bureau of Investigation

(FBI), where he served as a senior executive. His responsibilities at the FBI included a term as acting chief technology officer, section chief responsible for the FBI's technical collection and analysis platforms, and as a section chief overseeing the FBI's Cyber Division components responsible for the technical analysis of computer and network intrusion activities. His Cyber Division oversight included areas of malicious code analysis, computer exploitation tool reverse-engineering, and technical analysis of computer intrusions.